STEP-BY-STEP
Parts of Speech

LINWORTH LEARNING

From the Minds of Teachers

Linworth Publishing, Inc.
Worthington, Ohio

Cataloging-in-Publication Data

Editor: Claire Morris

Design and Production: Good Neighbor Press, Inc.

Published by Linworth Publishing, Inc.
480 East Wilson Bridge Road, Suite L
Worthington, Ohio 43085

ISBN: 1-58683-148-8

5 4 3 2

Table of Contents

Nouns

Nouns Name People 1
Nouns Name Places 2
Nouns Name Things 3
More Nouns Name Things 4
Sorting Nouns. 5
Plural People, Places, and Things. 6
Plural Nouns. 7
One or More?. 8
Singular and Plural Nouns 9
Reflect and Review. 10

Verbs

Identifying Verbs 11
More Identifying Verbs 12
Verbs at Home 13
Verbs in the Kitchen 14
Present Tense Verbs. 15
Which Verb? 16
Past Tense Verbs 17
Past Tense Verb Maze 18
Present and Past Tense Verbs. 19
Subject-Verb Agreement. 20
Matching Nouns and Verbs. 21
Choosing the Verb. 22
Reflect and Review. 23

Articles

Introducing Articles 24
Article Puzzle 25
Articles on a Train 26
A or *An*? 27
Choosing the Article 28
More *A* or *An*? 29
Reflect and Review. 30

Assessments

Assessment 1 31
Assessment 2 32
Assessment 3 33
Assessment 4 34
Assessment 5 35
Assessment 6 36
Assessment 7 37
Assessment 8 38
Assessment 9 39

Answer Key 40

Introduction

Step-by-Step Parts of Speech is designed to motivate and engage students who may have difficulty with language. Skills are addressed in a variety of fun and interesting formats to accommodate individual learning styles. Each skill is introduced according to a developmental progression and at low readability levels to promote success and understanding. Activity sheets have clear and simple instructions, examples,and exercises which may include word manipulation, understanding pictorial cues, and problem-solving. Assessment activities follow the format of standardized tests and require students to eliminate incorrect options, choose the correct answer, and fill in the appropriate circle. The material in this book correlates with the national curriculum standards for Grades 1–2 and covers the following skills: identifying and correctly using singular and plural nouns, identifying and correctly using present and past tense verbs, and identifying and correctly using articles. An answer key is provided at the back of the book.

Name_____ Date_____

Nouns Name People

Directions:

Look at the picture.

Choose the correct noun from the choices below.

Write the word on the line.

People

man   girl   boy   grandma   baby

1. _grandma_   2. _____

3. _____

4. _____   5. _____

⭐ Nouns Name Places

Directions:

Look at the map.

Read each question.

Use the map to answer the questions.

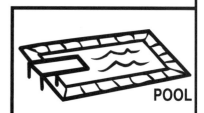

1. Where can people find many books? _____library_____

2. Where can people play outside? _____

3. Where can people swim? _____

4. Where can people live? _____

5. Where can people go to class? _____

6. Where can people buy something? _____

Nouns Name Things

Directions:

Look at the picture.

Choose the correct noun from the choices below.

Write the word on the line.

Things

mouth   ear   hair   leg   foot   arm   hand   nose

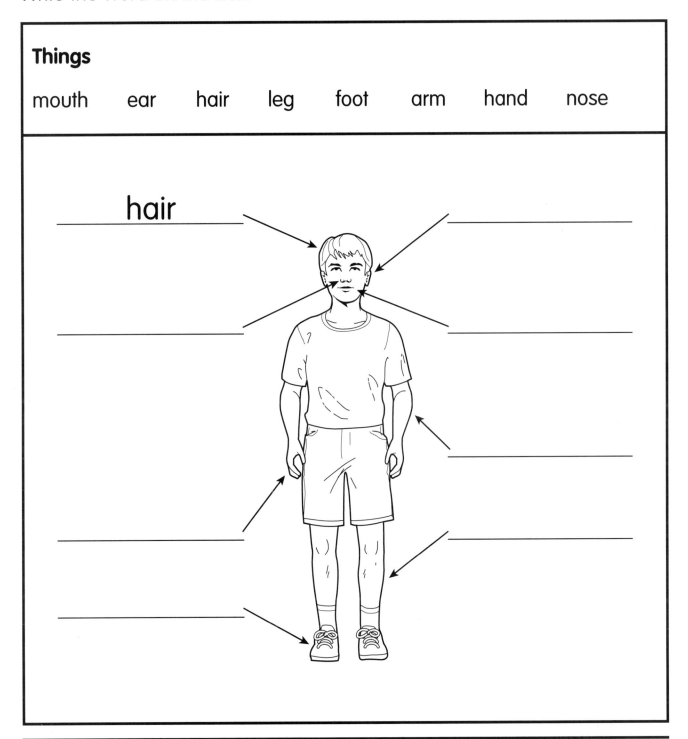

_____hair_____

More Nouns Name Things

Directions:

Look at the picture.

Choose the correct noun from the choices below.

Write the word on the line.

Things

ball   crab   sun   boat   shell

1. _____boat_____

2. _____

3. _____

4. _____

5. _____

Sorting Nouns

Directions:

Read each noun.

Cut out each noun, and glue it in the correct box.

People	Places	Things
boy	street	toy

man	frog	house
park	baby	girl
school	tree	fork

Plural People, Places, and Things

Directions:
Look at the picture.
Write the correct plural noun.
Draw a picture of the plural noun.

1. 	ant + s = ____ants____	
2. 	cat + s = _____	
3. 	bike + s = _____	
4. 	tree + s = _____	
5.	boat + s = _____	

Plural Nouns

Directions:
Read each group of words.
Write the correct plural noun.
Draw a picture of the plural noun.

1. one chick two ___chicks___	
2. one pig three _____	
3. one cow two _____	
4. one dog three _____	
5. one duck four _____	

One or More?

Directions:

Read the grocery list below.

Circle the correct nouns.

We need to buy:

1. four (apple, (apples))

2. two (pear, pears)

3. one (banana, bananas)

4. seven (grape, grapes)

5. three (orange, oranges)

6. six (egg, eggs)

Singular and Plural Nouns

Directions:

Look at the picture.

Choose the singular and plural nouns from the choices below.

Write the words in the correct columns.

Nouns

fish   crabs   cat   frog   birds   dogs

Singular Nouns (Only One)	**Plural Nouns** (More than One)
1. _____cat_____	1. _____
2. _____	2. _____
3. _____	3. _____

Reflect and Review

Directions:
Read each sentence.
Circle the singular nouns.
Draw a box around the plural nouns.

1. The (girl) eats two [cookies].

2. The woman reads two books.

3. The dogs bark at the bird.

4. The girls make a kite.

5. The man picks up three bags.

6. The cat plays with the toys.

Identifying Verbs

Directions:
Read each sentence, and look at the picture.
Choose the correct verb from the words below.
Write the word on the line.

Verbs

sings	talks	bakes	jumps	drives	reads

1. The moose ___drives___.

2. The moose _____.

3. The moose _____.

4. The moose _____.

5. The moose _____.

6. The moose _____.

More Identifying Verbs

Directions:
Look at each group of words.
Color the verb red.
Color the other words yellow.

1.
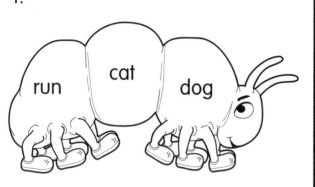
run cat dog

2.
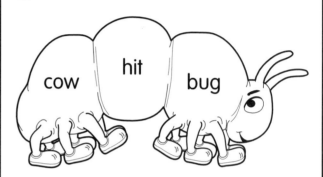
cow hit bug

3.
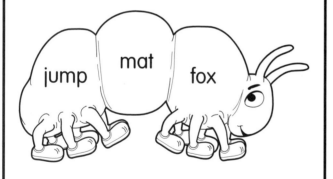
jump mat fox

4.
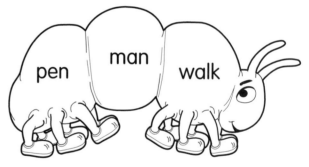
pen man walk

5.
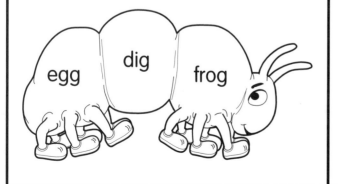
egg dig frog

6.
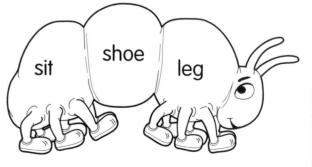
sit shoe leg

Verbs at Home

Directions:
Look at the picture.
Circle the people who are doing something.
Read each sentence.
Choose the correct verb from the choices below.
Write the word on the line.

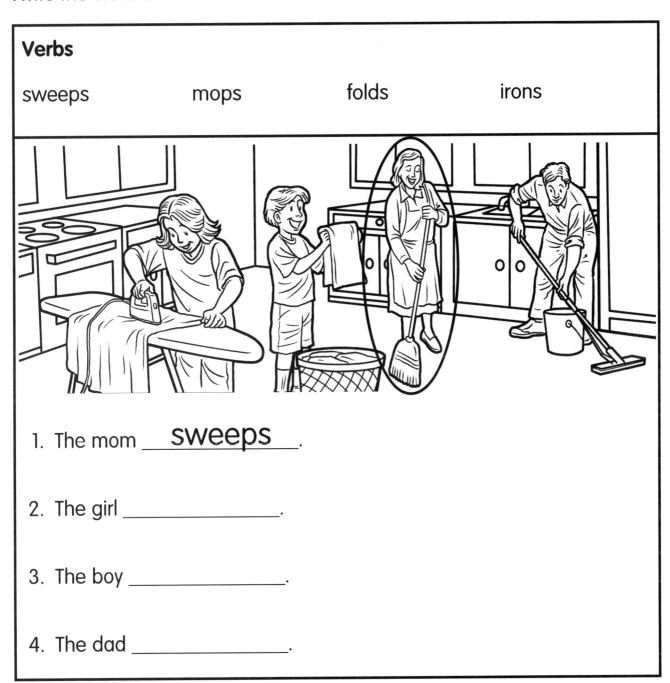

Verbs

sweeps	mops	folds	irons

1. The mom _____sweeps_____.

2. The girl _____.

3. The boy _____.

4. The dad _____.

Verbs in the Kitchen

Directions:
Read the information below.
Circle the verb in each sentence.
Then, draw a picture of a person making pudding.

How to Make Chocolate Pudding

I (open) the box of pudding.

I pour the mix into a bowl.

I measure three cups of milk.

I add the milk into the bowl.

I stir the pudding and milk.

I put it in the refrigerator.

I wait for it to cool.

I serve the pudding.

Present Tense Verbs

Directions:

Color the present tense verbs yellow.

Color the other words blue.

Write the verbs in the space below.

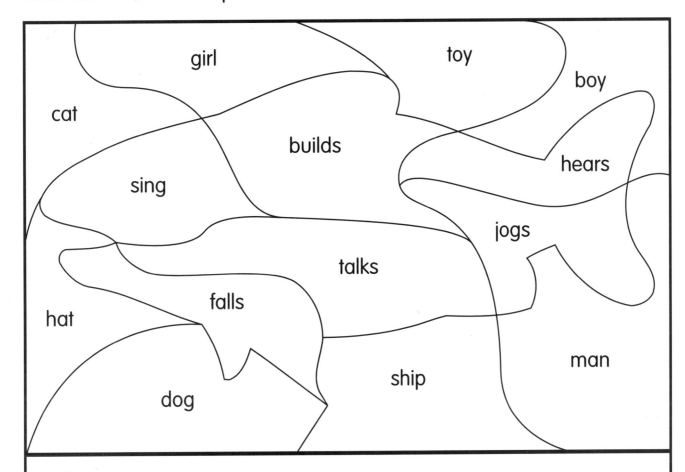

girl

toy

boy

cat

builds

hears

sing

jogs

talks

hat

falls

man

dog

ship

Verbs

sing _____

_____

_____

_____

Which Verb?

Directions:

Read each sentence.

Circle the correct verb.

1. The boy (jump, (jumps)) rope.

2. The girls (throw, throws) the ball.

3. The baby (sleep, sleeps) in the crib.

4. The dogs (run, runs) in the yard.

5. The flowers (grow, grows) in the garden.

6. The cat (sit, sits) in the chair.

Past Tense Verbs

Directions:

Match the shoes.

Draw a line from the present tense shoe to the correct past tense shoe.

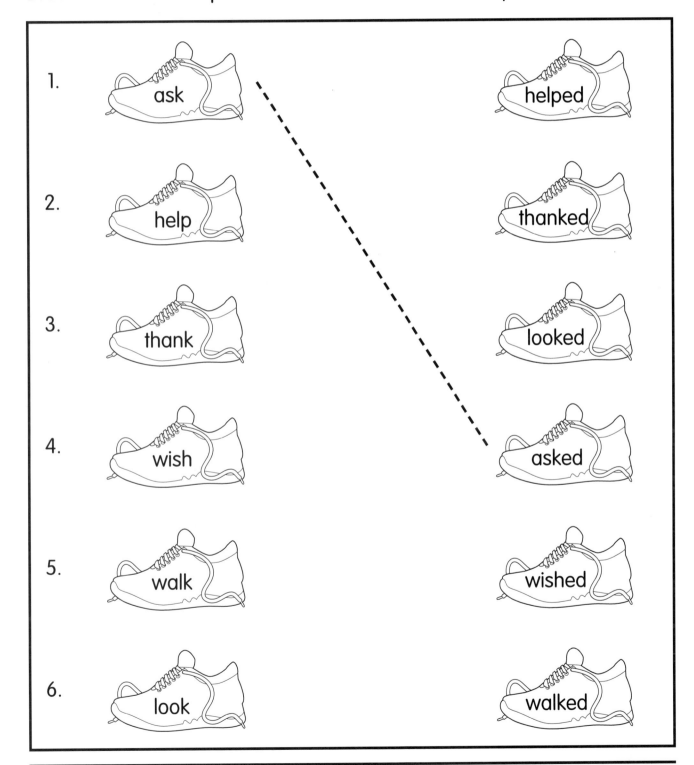

1. ask   helped

2. help   thanked

3. thank   looked

4. wish   asked

5. walk   wished

6. look   walked

Past Tense Verb Maze

Directions:

Follow the past tense verbs to finish the maze.
Help the baby ant find its family.

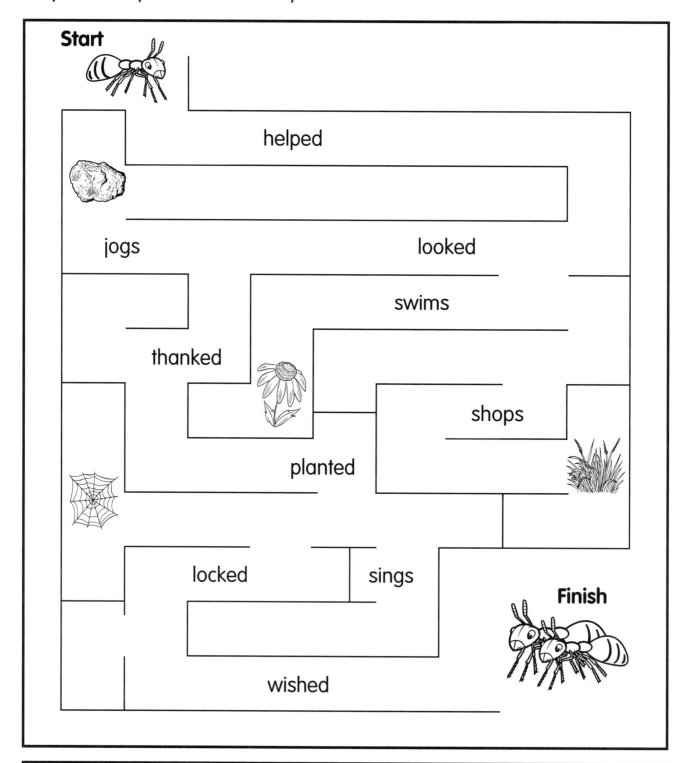

Start

helped

jogs   looked

swims

thanked

shops

planted

locked   sings

Finish

wished

Present and Past Tense Verbs

Directions:

Read each verb, and cut it out.

Decide if it is a present tense or past tense verb.

Glue the verb in the correct box.

Present Tense

Past Tense

 run

 played

 jumped

 throws

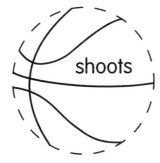 shoots

 helped

Subject-Verb Agreement

Directions:
Read each sentence, and look at the picture.
Circle the correct verb.

---

1. The  (look, (looks)) for food.

---

2. The  (play, plays) in the mud.

---

3. The  (sit, sits) in the nest.

---

4. The  (eat, eats) hay.

---

5. The  (climb, climbs) a tree.

Matching Nouns and Verbs

Directions:

Look at the pictures of the nouns, and read each verb.
Draw a line to the correct picture.

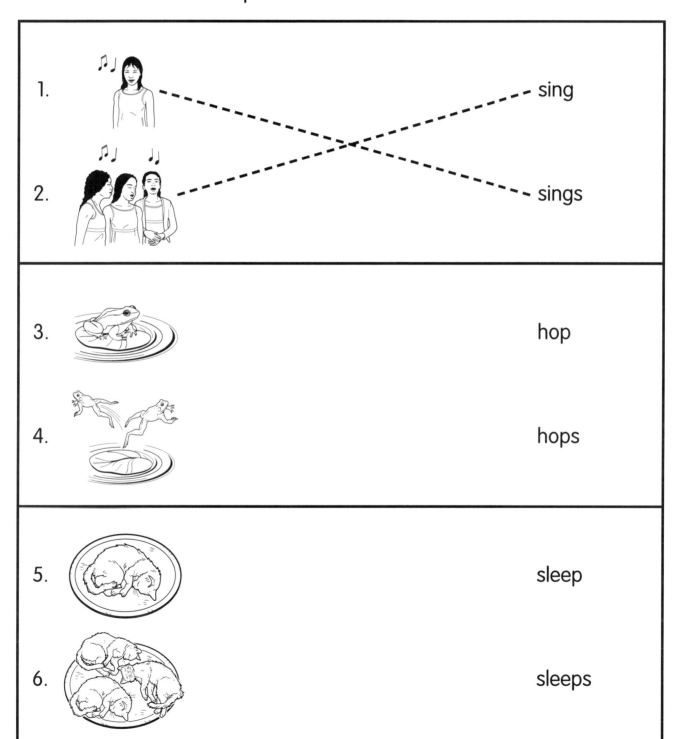

1. .... sing

2. .... sings

3. hop

4. hops

5. sleep

6. sleeps

Choosing the Verb

Directions:
Look at the pictures of the nouns, and read each verb.
Circle the correct verb.

1.		sing sings
2.		shine shines
3.		bark barks
4.		swim swims
5.		eat eats
6.		sleep sleeps

Reflect and Review

Directions:
Read each group of words.
Decide whether the group of words is a sentence.
If it is a sentence, circle yes.
Then, underline the nouns and circle the verb.
If it is not a sentence, circle no.

1. (Yes)   No   The <u>girls</u> (play).

2. Yes   No   The boys.

3. Yes   No   The baby takes a nap.

4. Yes   No   The woman reads a book.

5. Yes   No   Runs to the house.

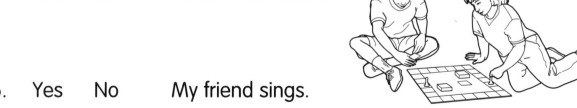

6. Yes   No   My friend sings.

Introducing Articles

Directions:
Read the poem.
Circle the articles.
Then, write the articles on the lines below.

There was (an) old woman

who swallowed a fly.

I don't know why

she swallowed the fly.

I think she'll cry!

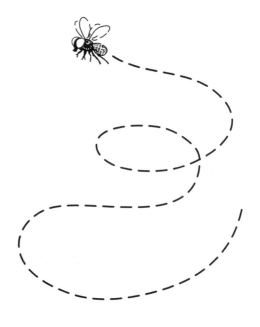

1. _____an_____

2. _____

3. _____

Article Puzzle

Directions:
Read each word.
If the word is an article, color the puzzle piece blue.
If the word is not an article, color the puzzle piece yellow.
Write the articles in the space below.

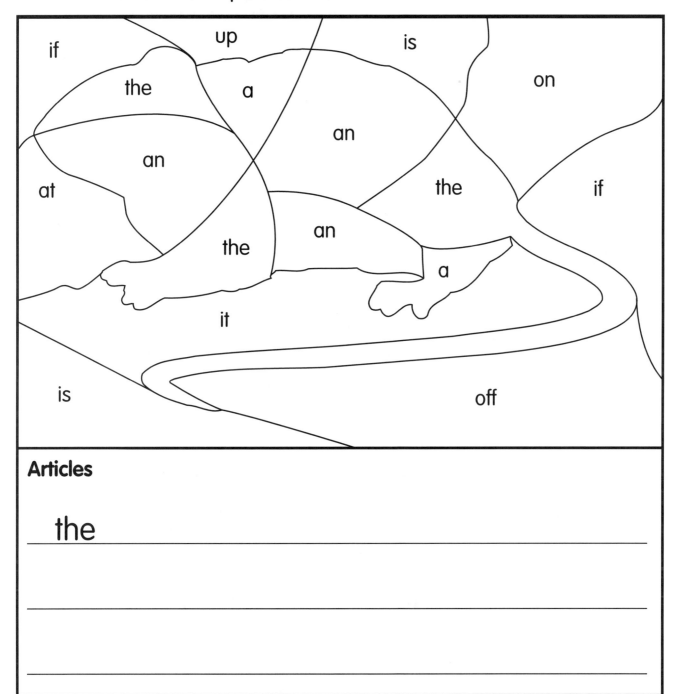

Articles

the
_____

_____

_____

Parts of Speech   **25**

Articles on a Train

Directions:

Read each word.

Write each word on a train car.

If the word is an article, color the train car yellow.

If the word is not an article, color the train car red.

Word box

a   at   of   an   the

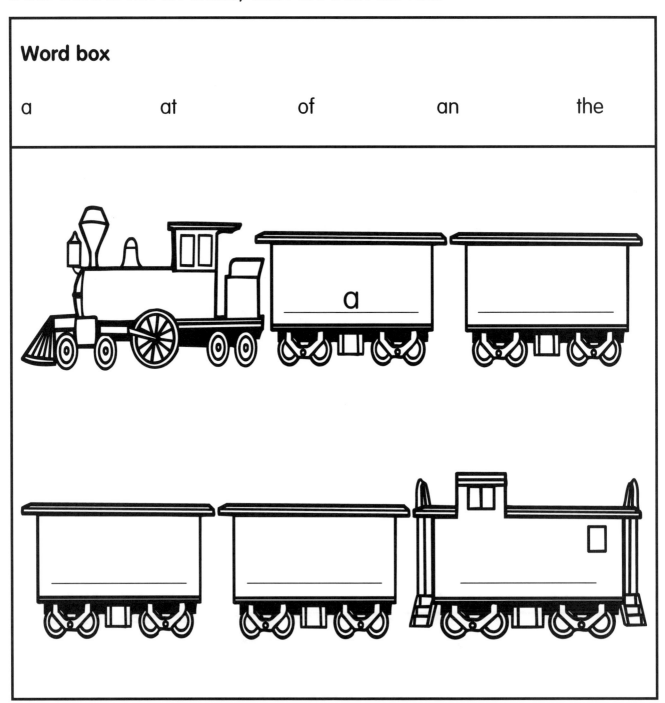

A or An?

Directions:

Look at each picture, and say what the picture is.

If the word begins with a consonant sound, write ***a***.

If the word begins with a vowel sound, write ***an***.

1. _____a_____

2. _____

3. _____

4. _____

5. _____

6. _____

Choosing the Article

Directions:

Look at the pictures in each box.

Circle the pictures that use the article.

a

an

⭐ More A or An?

Directions:
Read each sentence.
Circle the correct article.

---

1. My friend bakes (**a**), an) cake.

2. She adds (a, an) egg.

3. She pours (a, an) cup of milk in the bowl.

4. She stirs the batter with (a, an) spoon.

5. She puts it in (a, an) pan.

6. She bakes the cake in (a, an) oven.

Reflect and Review

Directions:

Read each noun.

Circle the correct article for each noun.

If the noun names only one, underline the noun once.

If the noun names more than one, underline the noun twice.

1. ((the), and) <u>dogs</u>

2. (a, an) ant

3. (a, an) pig

4. (a, an) tree

5. (a, an) owl

6. (a, the) flowers

Assessment 1

Directions:
Read each group of words.
Fill in the circle next to the noun.

1. ○ jump
   ○ climb
   ● boy

2. ○ girl
   ○ sing
   ○ play

3. ○ jog
   ○ walk
   ○ boy

4. ○ car
   ○ drive
   ○ say

5. ○ swim
   ○ sleep
   ○ house

Assessment 2

Directions:
Read each question.
Fill in the circle next to the correct answer.

---

1. Which noun names a place?

girl	fan	store
○	○	●

---

2. Which noun names a person?

frog	town	man
○	○	○

---

3. Which noun names a thing?

boy	dog	baby
○	○	○

---

4. Which noun names a place?

room	bed	toy
○	○	○

---

5. Which noun names a person?

house	pool	lady
○	○	○

---

6. Which noun names a thing?

bike	park	grandpa
○	○	○

Assessment 3

Directions:

Look at each picture.

Read each group of words.

Fill in the circle next to the correct answer.

| 1. | | ○ cat |
| | | ● cats |

| 2. | | ○ bike |
| | | ○ bikes |

| 3. | | ○ crab |
| | | ○ crabs |

| 4. | | ○ hat |
| | | ○ hats |

| 5. | | ○ school |
| | | ○ schools |

| 6. | | ○ tree |
| | | ○ trees |

Assessment 4

Directions:
Read each sentence.
Fill in the circle next to the correct answer.

1. The boy has two	○ book. ● books.
2. The dog finds one	○ bone. ○ bones.
3. The girl picks three	○ flower. ○ flowers.
4. The baby plays with one	○ toy. ○ toys.
5. The cat had two	○ kitten. ○ kittens.
6. The man has six	○ rock. ○ rocks.

Assessment 5

Directions:

Read each group of words.
Fill in the circle for the verb.

---

1. ○ kit   ● hit   ○ mitt

---

2. ○ bake   ○ cake   ○ lake

  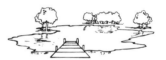

---

3. ○ jog   ○ log   ○ frog

---

4. ○ clip   ○ lip   ○ skip

 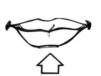

---

5. ○ throw   ○ bow   ○ crow

Assessment 6

Directions:

Read each sentence.

Fill in the circle next to the correct answer.

1.	Her cat _____ in the yard.	○ yells ○ swims ● runs
2.	The boy _____ for a snack.	○ looks ○ hides ○ runs
3.	He _____ a cookie.	○ tells ○ walks ○ eats
4.	The cat _____ in her lap.	○ talks ○ sleeps ○ stands
5.	His dad _____ him cookies.	○ bakes ○ jumps ○ sits

Assessment 7

Directions:
Read each sentence.
Fill in the circle next to the correct answer.

---

1. He _____ the dog.

   ○ kicked
   ○ played
   ● walked

---

2. She _____ the soccer ball.

   ○ yelled
   ○ parked
   ○ kicked

---

3. She _____ to her grandma.

   ○ packed
   ○ talked
   ○ climbed

---

4. He _____ up shells.

   ○ picked
   ○ jumped
   ○ walked

---

5. She _____ a flower.

   ○ barked
   ○ smelled
   ○ blocked

Assessment 8

Directions:

Look at each picture.

Fill in the circle under the correct article.

1.	a ○	an ●
2.	a ○	an ○
3.	a ○	an ○
4.	a ○	an ○
5.	a ○	an ○
6.	a ○	an ○

Assessment 9

Directions:

Read each nursery rhyme.

Circle the articles in each rhyme.

1. Little Miss Muffet

   Sat on (a) tuffet.

2. One, two buckle my shoe,

   Three, four shut the door.

3. Humpty Dumpty sat on a wall.

   Humpty Dumpty had a great fall.

4. There was an old who man

   Who lived in a shoe.

5. And the cow jumped over the moon.

   And the dish ran away with the spoon.

Nouns Name People

Directions:
Look at the picture.
Choose the correct noun from the choices below.
Write the word on the line.

People

man   girl   boy   grandma   baby

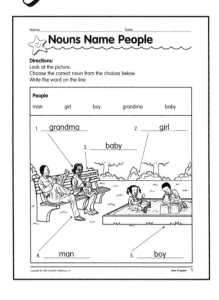

1. grandma
2. girl
3. baby
4. man
5. boy

Nouns Name Places

Directions:
Look at the map.
Read each question.
Use the map to answer the questions.

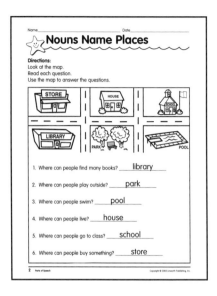

1. Where can people find many books? library
2. Where can people play outside? park
3. Where can people swim? pool
4. Where can people live? house
5. Where can people go to class? school
6. Where can people buy something? store

Nouns Name Things

Directions:
Look at the picture.
Choose the correct noun from the choices below.
Write the word on the line.

Things

mouth   ear   hair   leg   foot   arm   hand   nose

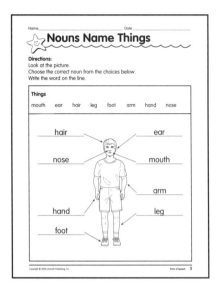

hair   ear
nose   mouth
arm
hand   leg
foot

More Nouns Name Things

Directions:
Look at the picture.
Choose the correct noun from the choices below.
Write the word on the line.

Things

ball   crab   sun   boat   shell

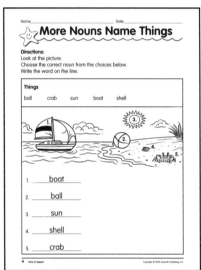

1. boat
2. ball
3. sun
4. shell
5. crab

Sorting Nouns

Directions:
Read each noun.
Cut out each noun, and glue it in the correct box.

People	Places	Things
boy	street	toy
man	park	tree
baby	school	frog
girl	house	fork

man	frog	house
park	baby	girl
school	tree	fork

Plural People, Places, and Things

Directions:
Look at the picture.
Write the correct plural noun.
Draw a picture of the plural noun.

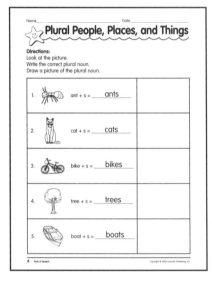

1. ant + s = ants
2. cat + s = cats
3. bike + s = bikes
4. tree + s = trees
5. boat + s = boats

Plural Nouns

Directions:
Read each group of words.
Write the correct plural noun.
Draw a picture of the plural noun.

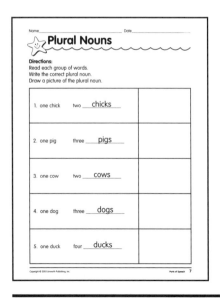

1. one chick   two chicks
2. one pig   three pigs
3. one cow   two cows
4. one dog   three dogs
5. one duck   four ducks

One or More?

Directions:
Read the grocery list below.
Circle the correct nouns.

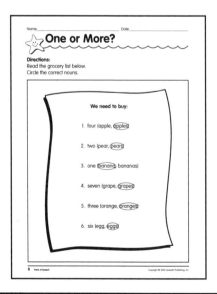

We need to buy:

1. four (apple, apples)
2. two (pear, pears)
3. one (banana, bananas)
4. seven (grape, grapes)
5. three (orange, oranges)
6. six (egg, eggs)

Singular and Plural Nouns

Directions:
Look at the picture.
Choose the singular and plural nouns from the choices below.
Write the words in the correct columns.

Nouns

fish   crabs   cat   frog   birds   dogs

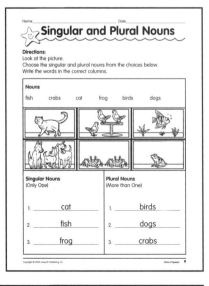

Singular Nouns (Only One)	Plural Nouns (More than One)
1. cat	1. birds
2. fish	2. dogs
3. frog	3. crabs

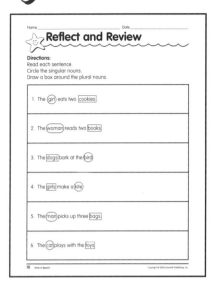

Reflect and Review

Directions:
Read each sentence.
Circle the singular nouns.
Draw a box around the plural nouns.

1. The (girl) eats two [cookies].

2. The (woman) reads two [books].

3. The [dogs] bark at the (bird).

4. The [girls] make a (kite).

5. The (man) picks up three [bags].

6. The (cat) plays with the [toys].

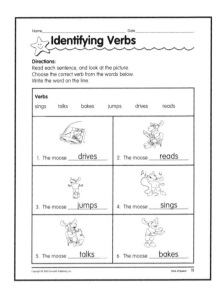

Identifying Verbs

Directions:
Read each sentence, and look at the picture.
Choose the correct verb from the words below.
Write the word on the line.

Verbs

sings   talks   bakes   jumps   drives   reads

1. The moose ___drives___   2. The moose ___reads___

3. The moose ___jumps___   4. The moose ___sings___

5. The moose ___talks___   6. The moose ___bakes___

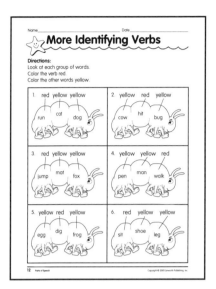

More Identifying Verbs

Directions:
Look at each group of words.
Color the verb red.
Color the other words yellow.

1. red yellow yellow
run   cat   dog

2. yellow red yellow
cow   hit   bug

3. red yellow yellow
jump   mat   fox

4. yellow yellow red
pen   man   walk

5. yellow red yellow
egg   dig   frog

6. red yellow yellow
sit   shoe   leg

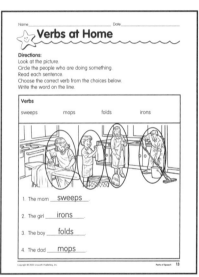

Verbs at Home

Directions:
Look at the picture.
Circle the people who are doing something.
Read each sentence.
Choose the correct verb from the choices below.
Write the word on the line.

Verbs

sweeps   mops   folds   irons

1. The mom ___sweeps___

2. The girl ___irons___

3. The boy ___folds___

4. The dad ___mops___

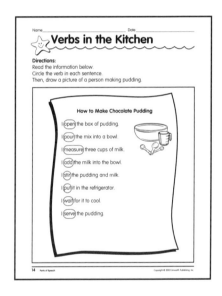

Verbs in the Kitchen

Directions:
Read the information below.
Circle the verb in each sentence.
Then, draw a picture of a person making pudding.

How to Make Chocolate Pudding

I (open) the box of pudding.
I (pour) the mix into a bowl.
I (measure) three cups of milk.
I (add) the milk into the bowl.
I (stir) the pudding and milk.
I (put) it in the refrigerator.
I (wait) for it to cool.
I (serve) the pudding.

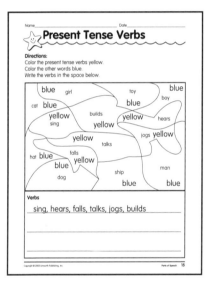

Present Tense Verbs

Directions:
Color the present tense verbs yellow.
Color the other words blue.
Write the verbs in the space below.

blue   girl   toy   blue
cat   blue   blue   boy
yellow   builds   yellow   hears
sing   yellow
yellow   jogs yellow
yellow   talks
hat   blue   falls
blue   yellow   man
dog   ship   blue   blue

Verbs

sing, hears, falls, talks, jogs, builds

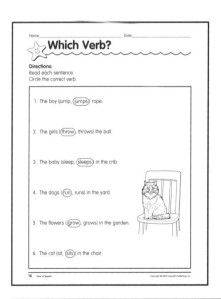

Which Verb?

Directions:
Read each sentence.
Circle the correct verb.

1. The boy (jump, (jumps)) rope.

2. The girls ((throw), throws) the ball.

3. The baby (sleep, (sleeps)) in the crib.

4. The dogs ((run), runs) in the yard.

5. The flowers ((grow), grows) in the garden.

6. The cat (sit, (sits)) in the chair.

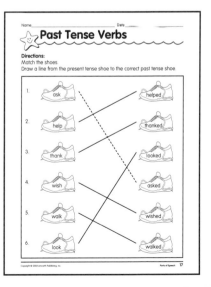

Past Tense Verbs

Directions:
Match the shoes.
Draw a line from the present tense shoe to the correct past tense shoe.

1. ask — helped
2. help — thanked
3. thank — looked
4. wish — asked
5. walk — wished
6. look — walked

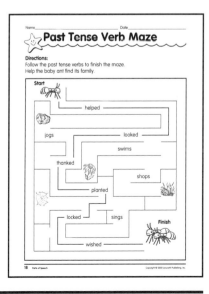

Past Tense Verb Maze

Directions:
Follow the past tense verbs to finish the maze.
Help the baby ant find its family.

Start
helped
jogs   looked
swims
thanked
shops
planted
locked   sings
Finish
wished

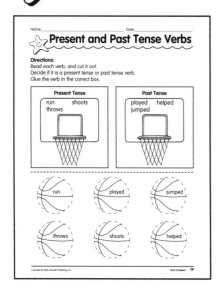

Present and Past Tense Verbs

Directions:
Read each verb, and cut it out.
Decide if it is a present tense or past tense verb.
Glue the verb in the correct box.

Present Tense
run shoots
throws

Past Tense
played helped
jumped

run played jumped
throws shoots helped

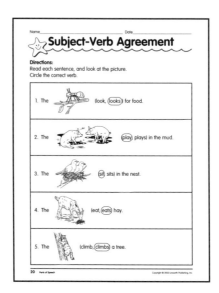

Subject-Verb Agreement

Directions:
Read each sentence, and look at the picture.
Circle the correct verb.

1. The (look, looks) for food.
2. The (play, plays) in the mud.
3. The (sit, sits) in the nest.
4. The (eat, eats) hay.
5. The (climb, climbs) a tree.

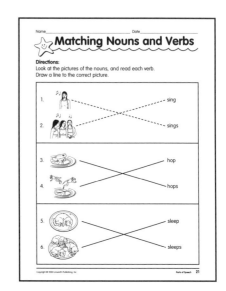

Matching Nouns and Verbs

Directions:
Look at the pictures of the nouns, and read each verb.
Draw a line to the correct picture.

1. — sing
2. — sings
3. — hop
4. — hops
5. — sleep
6. — sleeps

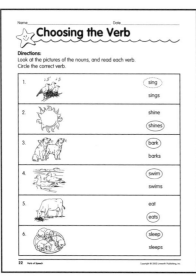

Choosing the Verb

Directions:
Look at the pictures of the nouns, and read each verb.
Circle the correct verb.

1. sing / sings
2. shine / shines
3. bark / barks
4. swim / swims
5. eat / eats
6. sleep / sleeps

Reflect and Review

Directions:
Read each group of words.
Decide whether the group of words is a sentence.
If it is a sentence, circle yes.
Then, underline the nouns and circle the verb.
If it is not a sentence, circle no.

1. Yes No The girls play.
2. Yes No The boys.
3. Yes No The baby takes a nap.
4. Yes No The woman reads a book.
5. Yes No Runs to the house.
6. Yes No My friend sings.

Introducing Articles

Directions:
Read the poem.
Circle the articles on the lines below.
Then, write the articles on the lines below.

There was an old woman
who swallowed a fly.
I don't know why
she swallowed the fly.
I think she'll cry!

1. _an_
2. _a_
3. _the_

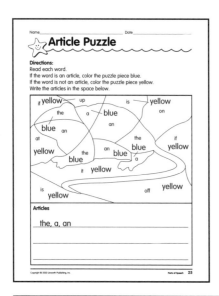

Article Puzzle

Directions:
Read each word.
If the word is an article, color the puzzle piece blue.
If the word is not an article, color the puzzle piece yellow.
Write the articles in the space below.

if yellow up is yellow
the a blue on
blue an an
at the if
yellow an blue yellow
blue the blue
it yellow
is off
yellow yellow

Articles
the, a, an

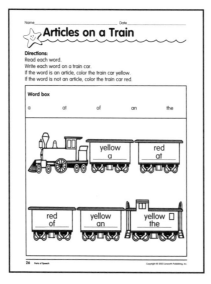

Articles on a Train

Directions:
Read each word.
Write each word on a train car.
If the word is an article, color the train car yellow.
If the word is not an article, color the train car red.

Word box
a   at   of   an   the

yellow a red at
red of yellow an yellow the

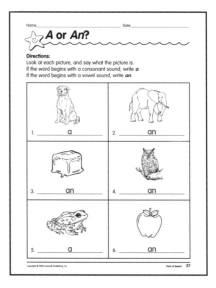

A or An?

Directions:
Look at each picture, and say what the picture is.
If the word begins with a consonant sound, write *a*.
If the word begins with a vowel sound, write *an*.

1. a   2. an
3. an   4. an
5. an

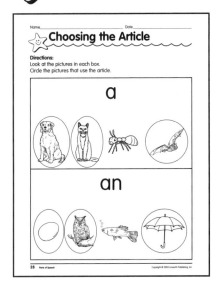

Name_____ Date_____
★ Choosing the Article

Directions:
Look at the pictures in each box.
Circle the pictures that use the article.

a

an

28 Parts of Speech   Copyright © 2003 Linworth Publishing, Inc.

Name_____ Date_____
★ More *A* or *An*?

Directions:
Read each sentence.
Circle the correct article.

1. My friend bakes (a, an) cake.

2. She adds (a, an) egg.

3. She pours (a, an) cup of milk in the bowl.

4. She stirs the batter with (a, an) spoon.

5. She puts it in (a, an) pan.

6. She bakes the cake in (a, an) oven.

Copyright © 2003 Linworth Publishing, Inc.   Parts of Speech 29

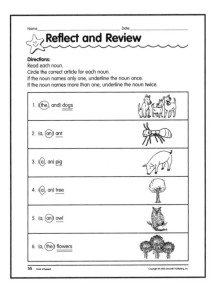

Name_____ Date_____
★ Reflect and Review

Directions:
Read each noun.
Circle the correct article for each noun.
If the noun names only one, underline the noun once.
If the noun names more than one, underline the noun twice.

1. (the, and) dogs

2. (a, an) ant

3. (a, an) pig

4. (a, an) tree

5. (a, an) owl

6. (a, the) flowers

30 Parts of Speech   Copyright © 2003 Linworth Publishing, Inc.

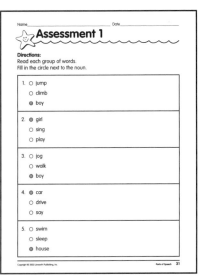

Name_____ Date_____
★ Assessment 1

Directions:
Read each group of words.
Fill in the circle next to the noun.

1. ○ jump
   ○ climb
   ● boy

2. ● girl
   ○ sing
   ○ play

3. ○ jog
   ○ walk
   ● boy

4. ● car
   ○ drive
   ○ say

5. ○ swim
   ○ sleep
   ● house

Copyright © 2003 Linworth Publishing, Inc.   Parts of Speech 31

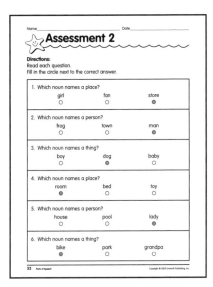

Name_____ Date_____
★ Assessment 2

Directions:
Read each question.
Fill in the circle next to the correct answer.

1. Which noun names a place?
   girl   fan   store
   ○   ○   ●

2. Which noun names a person?
   frog   town   man
   ○   ○   ●

3. Which noun names a thing?
   boy   dog   baby
   ○   ●   ○

4. Which noun names a place?
   room   bed   toy
   ●   ○   ○

5. Which noun names a person?
   house   pool   lady
   ○   ○   ●

6. Which noun names a thing?
   bike   park   grandpa
   ●   ○   ○

32 Parts of Speech   Copyright © 2003 Linworth Publishing, Inc.

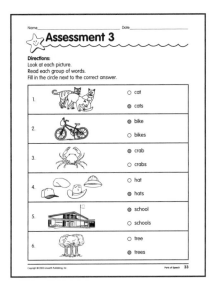

Name_____ Date_____
★ Assessment 3

Directions:
Look at each picture.
Read each group of words.
Fill in the circle next to the correct answer.

1. ○ cat
   ● cats

2. ● bike
   ○ bikes

3. ● crab
   ○ crabs

4. ● hat
   ○ hats

5. ● school
   ○ schools

6. ○ tree
   ● trees

Copyright © 2003 Linworth Publishing, Inc.   Parts of Speech 33

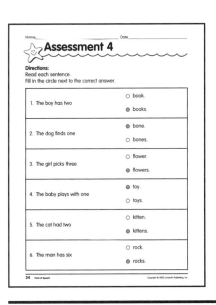

Name_____ Date_____
★ Assessment 4

Directions:
Read each sentence.
Fill in the circle next to the correct answer.

1. The boy has two
   ○ book.
   ● books.

2. The dog finds one
   ● bone.
   ○ bones.

3. The girl picks three
   ○ flower.
   ● flowers.

4. The baby plays with one
   ● toy.
   ○ toys.

5. The cat had two
   ○ kitten.
   ● kittens.

6. The man has six
   ○ rock.
   ● rocks.

34 Parts of Speech   Copyright © 2003 Linworth Publishing, Inc.

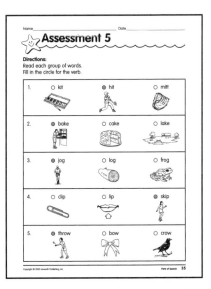

Name_____ Date_____
★ Assessment 5

Directions:
Read each group of words.
Fill in the circle for the verb.

1. ○ kit   ● hit   ○ mitt

2. ● bake   ○ cake   ○ lake

3. ● jog   ○ log   ○ frog

4. ○ clip   ○ lip   ● skip

5. ● throw   ○ bow   ○ crow

Copyright © 2003 Linworth Publishing, Inc.   Parts of Speech 35

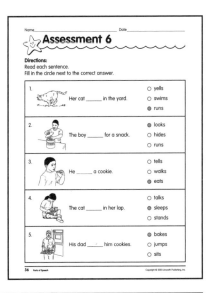

Name_____ Date_____
★ Assessment 6

Directions:
Read each sentence.
Fill in the circle next to the correct answer.

1. Her cat _____ in the yard.
   ○ yells
   ○ swims
   ● runs

2. The boy _____ for a snack.
   ● looks
   ○ hides
   ○ runs

3. He _____ a cookie.
   ○ tells
   ○ walks
   ● eats

4. The cat _____ in her lap.
   ○ talks
   ● sleeps
   ○ stands

5. His dad _____ him cookies.
   ● bakes
   ○ jumps
   ○ sits

36 Parts of Speech   Copyright © 2003 Linworth Publishing, Inc.

Answer Key pages 37–39

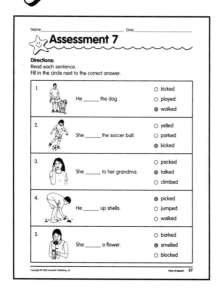

Assessment 7

Directions:
Read each sentence.
Fill in the circle next to the correct answer.

1.	He _____ the dog.	○ kicked ○ played ● walked
2.	She _____ the soccer ball.	○ yelled ○ parked ● kicked
3.	She _____ to her grandma.	● packed ● talked ○ climbed
4.	He _____ up shells.	● picked ○ jumped ○ walked
5.	She _____ a flower.	○ barked ● smelled ○ blocked

Copyright © 2003 Linworth Publishing, Inc.   Parts of Speech   **37**

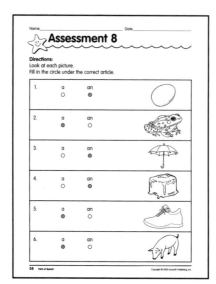

Assessment 8

Directions:
Look at each picture.
Fill in the circle under the correct article.

1.	a ○	an ●	
2.	a ●	an ○	
3.	a ○	an ●	
4.	a ○	an ●	
5.	a ●	an ○	
6.	a ●	an ○	

38   Parts of Speech   Copyright © 2003 Linworth Publishing, Inc.

Assessment 9

Directions:
Read each nursery rhyme.
Circle the articles in each rhyme.

1. Little Miss Muffet
   Sat on (a) tuffet.
2. One, two buckle my shoe,
   Three, four shut (the) door.
3. Humpty Dumpty sat on (a) wall.
   Humpty Dumpty had (a) great fall.
4. There was (an) old who man
   Who lived in (a) shoe.
5. And (the) cow jumped over (the) moon.
   And (the) dish ran away with (the) spoon.

Copyright © 2003 Linworth Publishing, Inc.   Parts of Speech   **39**